THE 10

Most Incredible Landforms

Mark John Lambert

Series Editor
Jeffrey D. Wilhelm

Much thought, debate, and research went into choosing and ranking the 10 items in each book in this series. We realize that everyone has his or her own opinion of what is most significant, revolutionary, amazing, deadly, and so on. As you read, you may agree with our choices, or you may be surprised — and that's the way it should be!

an imprint of

SCHOLASTIC

www.scholastic.com/librarypublishing

A Rubicon book published in association with Scholastic Inc.

Ru'bicon © 2008 Rubicon Publishing Inc.
www.rubiconpublishing.com

Associate Publishers: Kim Koh, Miriam Bardswich
Project Editor: Amy Land
Editors: Jessica Calleja, Linda Hughes
Creative Director: Jennifer Drew
Project Manager/Designer: Jeanette MacLean
Graphic Designer: Brandon Köpke

The publisher gratefully acknowledges the following for permission to reprint copyrighted material in this book.

Every reasonable effort has been made to trace the owners of copyrighted material and to make due acknowledgment. Any errors or omissions drawn to our attention will be gladly rectified in future editions.

"Crazy theories that turned out to be true" by Rachel Dickinson. First appeared in *The Christian Science Monitor*.

"Shipton's Arch Adventure," permission courtesy ©Ray Millar/The Natural Arch and Bridge Society.

"Jimmie Angel's Discovery of Angel Falls," from an article by Karen Angel. Permission courtesy Jimmie Angel Historical Project, April 5, 2007.

"How Deep is the Ocean?" An article from *Canada & The World Backgrounder*, January 2005. Reprinted with permission from *Canada & the World*, Waterloo, Ontario.

Cover: The Wave–© Arny Raedts/Arnyzona Photography

Library and Archives Canada Cataloguing in Publication

Lambert, Mark John, 1979–
  The 10 most incredible landforms / Mark John Lambert.

Includes index.
ISBN 978-1-55448-529-1

  1. Readers (Elementary). 2. Readers—Nature. I. Title.
II. Title: Ten most incredible landforms.

PE1117.L35 2007a   428.6   C2007-906701-8

1 2 3 4 5 6 7 8 9 10   10   17 16 15 14 13 12 11 10 09 08

Printed in Singapore

Contents

18

26

38

FROM THE GROUND UP

We live on an amazing planet. Just think — deep inside Earth's core is an extremely hot spinning ball of liquid iron and rock. Forces like heat, pressure, erosion, and gravity are all working together to shape our planet. Because of these many natural forces at work, our planet is constantly changing. The built-up pressure inside Earth is what made volcanoes erupt and continental plates shift millions of years ago, creating the amazing landforms that we see today. Millions of years from now, the spot where your home rests may be under a huge inland sea. Or a mountain may exist right where you are sitting at this very moment.

Think about it! Jagged mountains that touch the clouds; canyons that span for miles; trenches that cut so deeply the sun cannot reach them; and volcanic rivers that flow with molten rocks — these are just a few of the most amazing landforms that exist on our planet. You might read about them or see them on television, but imagine being there. Wouldn't that blow your mind?

In this book, we present what we think are the 10 most incredible landforms on our planet. We ranked them based on their size, physical features, and location. We also considered how rare they are, how they shape the landscape, how important they are as habitats, and how they affect people living in the area. Geologists are scientists who study how the Earth is formed. These are things they consider when studying landforms.

So pack your bags, grab your camera, and let's explore the world. Think like a geologist and ask yourself:

WHAT IS THE WORLD'S MOST INCREDIBLE LANDFORM?

10 OKOTOKS ERR

You can see how big this rock really is when you compare it to the group of people.

BIG ROCK–©BOB AIRHART

ATIC

WHERE? South of Calgary, Alberta, Canada

HOW BIG? About 130 ft. long, 60 ft. wide, and 30 ft. high

WOW FACTOR! Okotoks Erratic, also known as Big Rock, is the world's largest glacial erratic.

When you first see Okotoks Erratic, you will probably wonder how it got there. Almost three stories high, it stands out prominently against the flat prairie land. And this glacial erratic is huge — it weighs about 16,500 tons.

Take a step back and you will see that this mammoth boulder is part of a group of rocks. These rocks form a pattern stretching all the way from the town of Okotoks in Alberta, Canada, to northern Montana in the United States, a distance of over 430 miles.

Okotoks Erratic is made of an extremely hard and durable rock, similar to some of the rocks found in the Rocky Mountains near Jasper, Alberta. But Jasper is 250 miles to the northwest of Okotoks. So how could such a huge rock travel this distance? Simple — it hitched a ride. Read on to find out why Okotoks Erratic kicks off our list at #10.

glacial erratic: piece of rock carried by a glacier to a different landscape far away

OKOTOKS ERRATIC

THAT'S INCREDIBLE!

Erratic boulders are rocks that have been moved from their original location. Thousands of years ago, a large portion of Earth was covered with sheets of ice called glaciers. When the glaciers started to melt, they moved back. Large pieces of rock called boulders would break off the mountains and catch rides on these glaciers. These rocks were often carried long distances and left in faraway and unusual places. That's how a huge boulder like Okotoks Erratic ended up in a town so far away from its original home.

Quick Fact

Scientists believe there have been many Ice Ages in our past. The last Ice Age ended about 10,000 years ago.

Sunset Glow Boulder is the largest erratic boulder in the glaciation area of northern Europe.

FORCES AT WORK

The Rocky Mountains were formed around 600 million years ago. These mountains were originally sandstone, which is a sedimentary rock. The sandstone was exposed to heat and pressure and after millions of years was compacted and turned into quartzite, which is a very hard and durable rock. The surface became smooth as the rock was eroded by water. Ice started to work its way into small cracks in the rock, freezing and expanding. This caused large sections to break off. One of these pieces was Okotoks Erratic.

INSIDE OUT

Erratic boulders, like all rocks, are typically made up of one or a combination of three types of rock: sedimentary, igneous, and metamorphic. Sedimentary rocks form when extreme pressure is applied to very small particles of rock or various materials over many years. Igneous rocks form when magma and lava (which come from volcanoes) cool on or near Earth's surface. Metamorphic rocks form when either sedimentary rocks and/or igneous rocks are exposed to intense heat and pressure.

eroded: *worn away*

? What other things in nature do you think could have been carried or moved by glaciers? Make a list.

Crazy Theories
that turned out to be true

Article from *The Christian Science Monitor*
By Rachel J. Dickinson, September 11, 2004

Baby, it's coooold outside: The Great Ice Age

Many years ago — 167 years ago, to be exact — a Swiss naturalist named Louis Agassiz (Ag-uhs-see) proposed the theory of the Great Ice Age. Agassiz grew up in the Swiss Alps and was very familiar with alpine (mountain) glaciers and their effects on the landscape. One day two of his friends took him to see an alpine glacier and pointed out big boulders (called erratics) strewn across a valley well below the glacier. Agassiz and his friends recognized that these huge boulders must have been carried into the valley by a strong force — a glacier. But how could that be? The glacier was way up the mountainside.

Then Agassiz's friends pointed to ridges of gravel, sand, and boulders that marked the front edge of where a glacier had once stood. At that time, naturalists who studied glaciers knew that these very slow moving "ice rivers" scoured the land beneath them. They also picked up and carried everything in their path.

And because of the way the ice in a glacier moves, any debris that a glacier has picked up will be deposited at the front edge of a glacier. That's what creates these ridges of material, called moraines.

This was a "Eureka!" moment for Agassiz. Suddenly, everywhere he looked he saw evidence that glaciers had been there. He saw erratics where they shouldn't be, far from the bedrock from which they had broken off. He saw glacial moraines where others just saw gravel banks. In places like Scotland, which is thousands of miles from the nearest glacier, Agassiz saw rocks with long striations — scratches or gouges — on them. The striations indicated the presence of a once flowing glacier.

---

naturalist: *scientist who studies nature*
moraines: *rocks, stones, and soil carried and deposited by a glacier*

 What do you think it feels like to make an amazing discovery and have a "Eureka" moment?

The Expert Says...

"Geologists study glacial erratics to learn more about the way continental glaciers work. ... Some erratics have been moved several hundred kilometers [miles] from their source."

— Alec Aitken, associate professor of geography, University of Saskatchewan

Take Note

Okotoks Erratic, the largest glacial erratic on Earth, rolls in at #10 on our list. Erratic boulders give us clues about Earth's history and the forces of erosion and glacial action. They are an interesting landform, but they are not rare.

• What information about Earth's history can we get from studying the movement of erratic boulders?

5   4   3   2   1

This picture of Shipton's Arch shows the powerful effects of water in creating amazing landforms.

CH

WHERE? Northwest of Kashgar, China

HOW BIG? Over 1,200 ft. tall (about the height of the Empire State Building!), with a span of about 180 ft.

WOW FACTOR! It is the highest natural bridge in the world!

Think about the many types of bridges in the world. There are suspended bridges, bridges supported by frameworks, and bridges set upon beams, to name a few. One type of bridge you might not be familiar with is a natural arch. This land formation is rare and fascinating. A natural arch is solid rock that has been worn away in weak places by weathering and erosion to create a naturally formed passageway.

The highest natural arch in China was known as *Tushuk Tash*. It was not known to the West until 1947 when it was discovered by British mountaineer Eric Shipton.

Today we call it Shipton's Arch. It made its way into the *Guinness Book of World Records* as the highest natural arch in the world. With this honor, Shipton's Arch easily takes the #9 spot on our list.

SHIPTON'S ARCH

THAT'S INCREDIBLE!

Shipton's Arch was introduced to the West in 1947. After that, its location was lost for several years because it is so hard to get to. Incredibly, it was rediscovered and featured in *National Geographic* in 2000. It has since regained its status as the world's highest natural arch. Today, several companies operate day trips for tourists. As the number of climbers increases, the ladders needed to reach the arch have been made permanent for these nature buffs.

FORCES AT WORK

Think about the forces of water, gravity, temperature, and pressure working away on rocks. Water washes away the small grains that hold a rock together. As these small grains are carried away by gravity, the crack that the water runs through gets deeper. As the seasons change and the water inside the cracks freezes and thaws, the rock contracts and expands. If this occurs along a tectonic plate line, there is a good chance the underground movement will cause pieces to break off, eventually forming an arch. Some arches form with the help of all four elements. Others might only need one or two (as long as water is one of them).

tectonic plate: *large piece of Earth's crust*

Quick Fact

Earth's crust is made up of seven large and many smaller moving tectonic plates. Their average annual movement is a few inches every year.

INSIDE OUT

Natural arches form in places where many different kinds of rocks exist together. Sedimentary rocks erode more quickly and easily. Igneous rocks erode very slowly and seem to take a very long time to change. Metamorphic rocks erode at varying rates. Shipton's Arch is made from a very crumbly conglomerate, which is a sedimentary rock made from smaller stones that have been packed together.

Crumbly conglomerate

? Do you think tourists should be visiting Shipton's Arch or do you think we should leave this natural wonder alone? Make a list of the pros and cons.

This view of the arch shows different types of rock that are exposed by water erosion.

SHIPTON'S ARCH ADVENTURE

Ray Millar of the Natural Arch and Bridge Society shares his journey to Shipton's Arch in this photo essay.

A couple of days before, a small group of us traveled to view the arch from the south side.

This is our camp site located near a slot canyon. Earlier it had rained in the area, increasing the danger of flooding.

We laddered our way up the slot canyon for about 145 feet to reach Tushuk Tash.

Here I am with the north side of the arch in the background. The upper part of the arch soared high above us, but the sides continued down and could not be seen.

 Would you ever want to explore Shipton's Arch? Why or why not?

The Expert Says...

"The top of the slope is very deceptive and drops dramatically away into the canyon."

— Ray Millar, member of the Natural Arch and Bridge Society

Take Note

Shipton's Arch takes the #9 spot. It is not only the highest natural bridge in the world, but its location is so remote that it was "lost" for several years before it was rediscovered. It's not every day you get to see one of these landforms and some people have never even heard of a natural arch.

• Water plays a role in the creation of both erratic boulders and natural arches. Compare how it is used in the creation of each.

5   4   3   2   1

The striations or linear markings on the rock surfaces make the landscape look like moving waves.

ES AND THE WAVE

WHERE? Monument Valley, Arizona, United States

HOW BIG? 985 ft. high on a base of almost 1,475 ft.

WOW FACTOR! This natural land formation looks like liquid rock!

When you hear the word "wave" you likely think of water. But have you ever seen a rock that looks like a wave? Located just south of the border between Utah and Arizona is a place that few people visit or even know about. It is a rough and dry landscape of swirling gullies, hills, cliffs, and odd creations of twisted sandstone rock. This place is filled with buttes — hills with very steep sides and flat tops — and is the home of the spectacular Coyote Buttes.

Coyote Buttes are multicolored rock formations. Deposits of iron in the rock create a rainbow of yellow, pink, and red colors. These buttes have sides that "flow like water" and they look as though they are moving. In the north section of the area is the Wave, a unique and spectacular piece of sculpted sandstone that is something out of this world. So, at first glance these unusual rocks may seem to belong on another planet, but they take the #8 spot as one of Earth's most amazing landforms.

COYOTE BUTTES AND THE WAVE

THAT'S INCREDIBLE!

The Coyote Buttes and the Wave were not known until the mid-1990s. The location is remote, and it is a difficult hike to get to the Wave. Once there, visitors are treated to a landscape that is out of this world. The patterns and colors of the rock formation change throughout the day and the season. Today, visitors require a permit because the eroding sedimentary rock makes these landforms very fragile. To protect from human damage, only 20 people are allowed to visit each day.

Quick Fact

Buttes don't rise out of the ground. They are the remains of higher land that has been weathered away and lowered by erosion.

FORCES AT WORK

The heat and movement generated from the spinning ball of molten rock and iron in Earth's core creates pressure that pushes up the land. This pushed-up land forms a plateau, which has a flat top and at least one steep side. As rainwater and streams flow over the edges of the plateau, erosion takes place. Water then cuts into the side of the plateau separating it into sections called *mesas* (a Spanish word meaning table mountains that are larger than buttes). After a few more thousand years, the softer rock under the cap erodes. Pieces of the cap rock then break away, forming a butte.

? What do you think erosion will do to a butte after another million years? What might the landscape look like?

INSIDE OUT

Most buttes are made of sedimentary rock that wears away easily. But they also have a "cap rock" on top that is made of harder rock, such as igneous, which is more resistant to erosion.

Quick Fact

Buttes are always eroding, but so slowly that you will probably not notice any changes in your lifetime.

The many layers of sedimentary rock as well as the harder cap rock forming the buttes can be seen here.

The Expert Says...

"The spectacular thing about buttes is that they stand out from the local landscape in pinnacle forms with their flat tops and steep sides.

— Dr. Les King, professor, School of Geography and Geology, McMaster University

pinnacle: *natural rocky peak*

10   9   8   7   6

MYSTERIOUS MARTIAN FACE

This article describes a strange discovery in outer space.

Back in 1976, a National Aeronautics and Space Administration (NASA) spacecraft was circling Mars and snapping photos when it spotted a shadowy likeness of a human face. An enormous head over two miles long from end-to-end seemed to be staring back from a part of Mars called Cydonia.

The "face" on Mars became famous. It was seen in movies, books, and magazines. Some people thought the face was proof of life on Mars, while others thought it was the remains of an ancient civilization.

In 2001, another NASA spacecraft was able to get close enough for another look. It was able to capture an extraordinary picture using a better camera than the one used in 1976. This time, they figured out the form was not a face. It is actually the Martian version of a butte,

a landform common in the American West. Planetary geologists are very interested in these buttes because they lie in transitional zones between cratered highlands to the south and smoother lowlands to the north of the planet. Some scientists think the northern plains are all that's left of an ancient ocean. So is it possible that Cydonia was a beach front property many millions of years ago?

? How important is the discovery of buttes on Mars? What does it tell you about the planet?

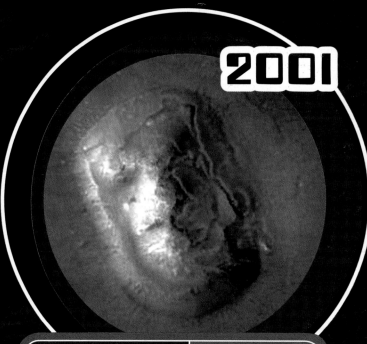

2001

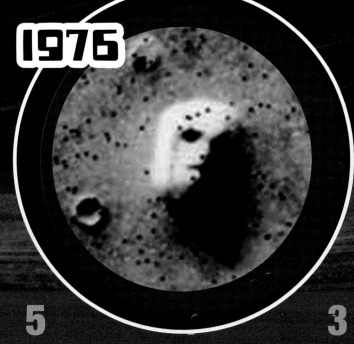

1976

Take Note

The Coyote Buttes and the Wave are spectacular landforms. But they are also very fragile and should be protected. Their unusual formation, their size, and their incredible appearance secure their #8 spot on our list.
• Do you think that the number of people visiting this site should be limited or do you think that more people should be allowed to visit? Explain your answer.

5   3   2   1

(7) ANGEL FALLS

Angel Falls is 15 times higher than the famous Niagara Falls. Niagara Falls is located on the border of New York State and Ontario.

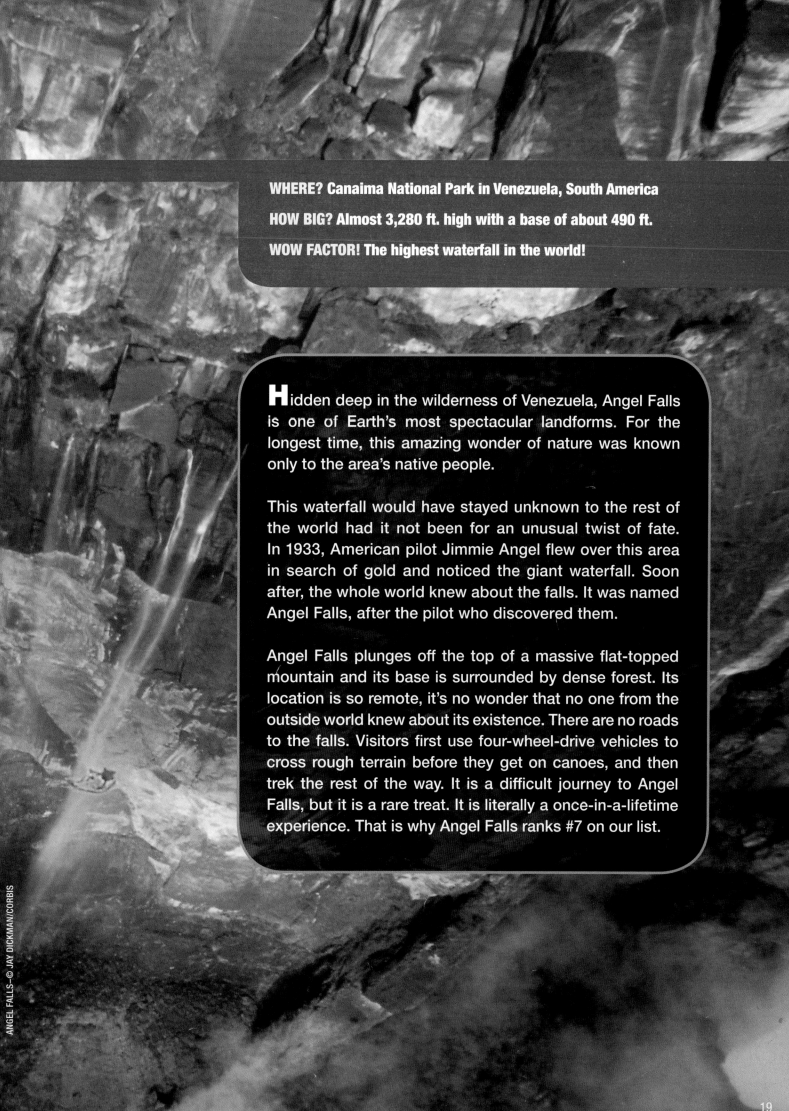

WHERE? Canaima National Park in Venezuela, South America

HOW BIG? Almost 3,280 ft. high with a base of about 490 ft.

WOW FACTOR! The highest waterfall in the world!

Hidden deep in the wilderness of Venezuela, Angel Falls is one of Earth's most spectacular landforms. For the longest time, this amazing wonder of nature was known only to the area's native people.

This waterfall would have stayed unknown to the rest of the world had it not been for an unusual twist of fate. In 1933, American pilot Jimmie Angel flew over this area in search of gold and noticed the giant waterfall. Soon after, the whole world knew about the falls. It was named Angel Falls, after the pilot who discovered them.

Angel Falls plunges off the top of a massive flat-topped mountain and its base is surrounded by dense forest. Its location is so remote, it's no wonder that no one from the outside world knew about its existence. There are no roads to the falls. Visitors first use four-wheel-drive vehicles to cross rough terrain before they get on canoes, and then trek the rest of the way. It is a difficult journey to Angel Falls, but it is a rare treat. It is literally a once-in-a-lifetime experience. That is why Angel Falls ranks #7 on our list.

ANGEL FALLS

THAT'S INCREDIBLE!

Angel Falls is located in the Canaima National Park, a place of unspoiled beauty, in Venezuela, South America. There are two ways to see the falls. You can either fly over or see it from ground level. You do this by taking a boat ride to the base. There are organized tours to Angel Falls from the town of Canaima.

FORCES AT WORK

A river collects rainwater falling on the Auyán Tepui (Au-yan Ta-pwe), the highest mountain in Venezuela, and directs it toward a high cliff. Tepuis are table-like mountains. They are some of the oldest land formations on the planet and are found only in the Guiana Highlands. From the top, the water falls uninterrupted for almost 3,280 feet to a swirling pool below. Imagine the silence broken by the sound of the crashing waterfall and the mist and spray that are created by the force of the water.

INSIDE OUT

The waterfall plunges over a rock cliff of sandstone and quartz. Over millions of years, erosion has slowly worn away layers of sandstone, exposing more of the harder quartz rock.

? Find out more about Angel Falls and Niagara Falls. How is the formation of these falls different or similar?

Quick Fact

Pemón are the native people of southeastern Venezuela. One-fourth of the 12,000 to 13,000 Pemón live in the Kamarata Valley in Canaima National Park. This is one of the largest parks in the world.

Quick Fact

The local Pemón people named the waterfall *Parekupa-meru*, which translates to "waterfall of the deepest place."

Airplane in flight above Auyán Tepui

10   9   7

JIMMIE ANGEL'S DISCOVERY OF ANGEL FALLS

Jimmie Angel's niece, Karen Angel, reports on her uncle's journey in this article.
— April 5, 2007

In 1933, American jungle pilot Jimmie Angel was searching for gold in the highlands of southeastern Venezuela. Flying solo, he was amazed to see a waterfall flowing from a massive tabletop mountain. He was even more amazed when it measured about 5,275 feet high on his airplane's altimeter. The mountain was called "Auyán Tepui." This means "Devil's Mountain" in the language of the area's native Pemón people. They believed evil spirits lived on the mountain because it was often covered with storm clouds.

Jimmie Angel and three other people landed on Auyán Tepui in 1937. The landing was perfect, but the airplane broke through the soft mossy ground and got stuck in mud. The party left the airplane and trekked for 11 days across Auyán Tepui to reach safety.

Scientific expeditions were organized to explore Auyán Tepui's natural environment. The waterfall was named "Angel Falls" in the 1940s because of writings that were inspired by Angel's explorations.

In 1949, American photojournalist Ruth Roberts led an expedition to the base of Angel Falls. She measured its height at 3,210 feet high with the first main drop at 2,645 feet. Her expedition was published that year in *National Geographic*.

---

altimeter: *instrument used to measure height above sea level*

Jimmie and his wife Marie Angel

Angel's Flamingo airplane is stuck in the bog atop Auyán Tepui.

The Expert Says...

" … naming the falls after Jimmie Angel makes it a monument to the courage and persistence of this explorer-aviator and soldier of fortune. "

— Dr. E. Thomas Gilliard, naturalist, American Museum of Natural History

Take Note

The Angel Falls is a natural wonder. It showcases a body of water plunging almost 3,280 feet from a flat-topped mountain. Its spectacular beauty, its size, and its remote location combine to secure its #7 spot on our list.

• Which would you rather visit — Coyote Buttes or Angel Falls? Explain your answer.

5   4   3   2   1

Mammoth Cave was made a UNESCO World Heritage site in 1981. This means the area is an important part of history and needs to be protected.

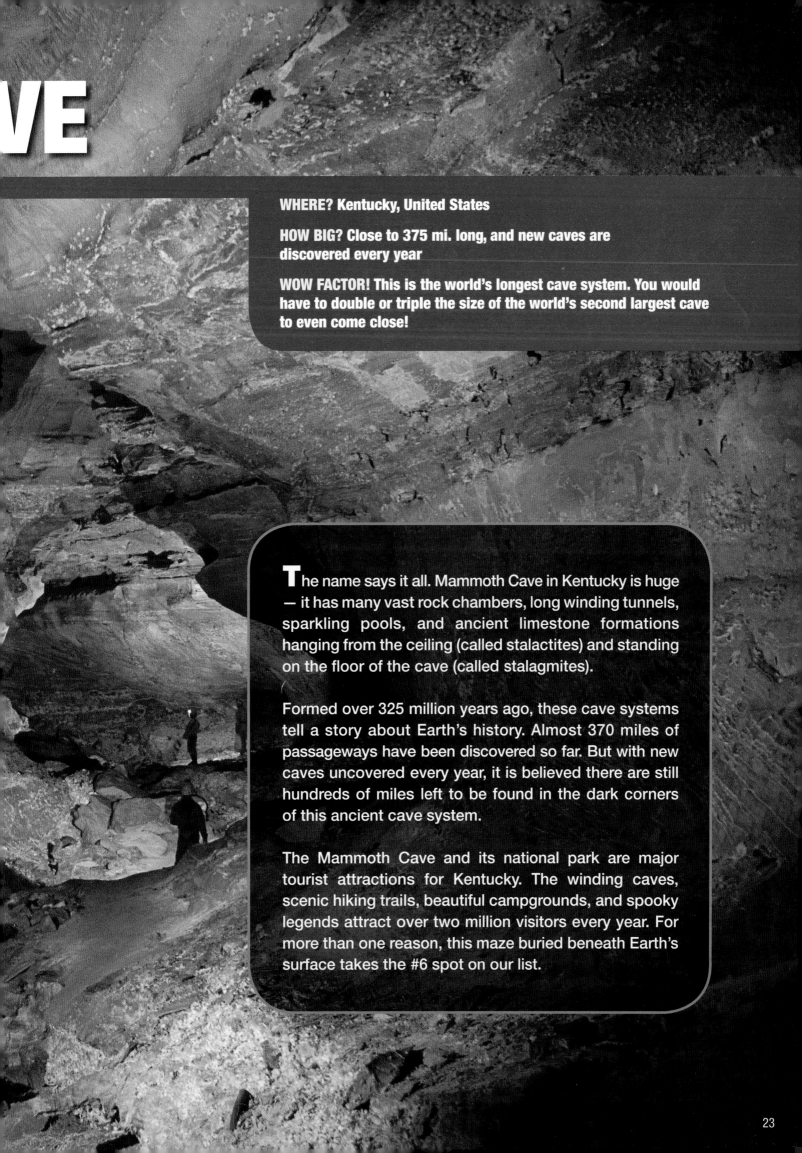

VE

WHERE? Kentucky, United States

HOW BIG? Close to 375 mi. long, and new caves are discovered every year

WOW FACTOR! This is the world's longest cave system. You would have to double or triple the size of the world's second largest cave to even come close!

The name says it all. Mammoth Cave in Kentucky is huge — it has many vast rock chambers, long winding tunnels, sparkling pools, and ancient limestone formations hanging from the ceiling (called stalactites) and standing on the floor of the cave (called stalagmites).

Formed over 325 million years ago, these cave systems tell a story about Earth's history. Almost 370 miles of passageways have been discovered so far. But with new caves uncovered every year, it is believed there are still hundreds of miles left to be found in the dark corners of this ancient cave system.

The Mammoth Cave and its national park are major tourist attractions for Kentucky. The winding caves, scenic hiking trails, beautiful campgrounds, and spooky legends attract over two million visitors every year. For more than one reason, this maze buried beneath Earth's surface takes the #6 spot on our list.

MAMMOTH CAVE

THAT'S INCREDIBLE!

Mammoth Cave System supports a wide diversity of species living in unique and interconnected ecosystems. The creatures that live in these caves include troglobites like eyeless fish (which live their whole lives within a cave), troglophiles like spiders (which live either inside or outside of caves), and trogloxenes like bats (which live in caves most of the time but leave for food).

---

ecosystems: *communities of animals, plants, and bacteria, including the environment where they live*

Quick Fact

Two hundred species of animals live inside the Mammoth Cave System. Twelve of these species have no eyes and no color.

Eyeless fish

? Why do you think that certain creatures living inside Mammoth Cave do not have eyes? How do you think they get around?

FORCES AT WORK

Millions of years ago, most of the American continent was covered by a huge sea. As marine creatures died, their decaying bodies built up a layer of limestone on the ocean floor. This layer became so thick that the ocean floor began to pile up and water started to move through this limestone layer, carving small caves. As years passed, Earth continued to shift and water was able to cut deeper into the limestone, carving a large cave system. Rivers deposited hard sandstone on top of the limestone and this preserved the caves. After millions of years, the water disappeared and left this large network.

INSIDE OUT

Mammoth Cave is made from limestone that formed between 360 and 325 million years ago. The limestone is capped by a layer of sandstone. This combination makes the system very stable.

Quick Fact

Limestone is a sedimentary rock made from the shells of dead sea creatures that lived millions of years ago.

Exploring Mammoth Cave

The Expert Says...

"Exploration and mapping are ongoing ... Mammoth Cave is 367 miles long right now, but no one knows its complete length – yet!"

— Vickie Carson, public information officer, Mammoth Cave National Park

The World's Most Haunted Place

Are you surprised that a place so old, so creepy, and so huge is surrounded by legends and mysterious tales? This article about the ghosts of Mammoth Cave is sure to make your hair stand on end.

Running Leg

While exploring alone in 1925, Floyd Collins became trapped underneath a heavy rock. He eventually died in the cave despite rescue attempts. Floyd's body was preserved in a glass-topped chest and displayed as a tourist attraction. It was later stolen and found in a field with only one leg. After this, he was finally buried on the national park grounds. It is said that a ghost still haunts the cave calling for "Johnny," who was Floyd's best friend. People have also reported seeing a leg running around. Many believe it is Floyd's missing leg searching for its owner.

Floyd Collins

Lost Love

A girl named Melissa fell in love with her tutor, a man named Beverleigh. When she found out Beverleigh loved someone else, she led him into the cave and left him there as revenge. He was never seen again. On her deathbed in 1858, Melissa confessed her act. Many believe that her spirit is wandering the cave looking for her tutor and that he is wandering the cave looking for a way out.

Wandering Ghost

Stephen Bishop was an African American who started exploring the cave in the 1830s. He loved the caves so much that he lived there his entire life. He died in 1857 and was buried on a hill near the cave entrance. Today, Stephen is seen wandering the caves. He is usually seen wearing a dark shirt, white pants, and slouch hat. Sometimes he actually joins tour groups, saying nothing but allowing himself to be seen.

Quick Fact

In 1990, Mammoth Cave was named an International Biosphere Reserve. This means the area must be used in ways that are friendly to the environment.

? Think like a geologist or cave explorer and find out more about Mammoth Cave and its national park. What would you most like to discover and why?

Take Note

The world's largest cave system is #6 on our list. It covers a large surface and it is home to many rare species of organisms. Nobody knows how big the cave system really is, as new caves are still being discovered. Plus, this landform attracts lots of tourists every year.

• Do you think there are any other landforms out there that have not been discovered? Where and what might they be?

5   4   3   2   1

5 MAUNA LOA

Mauna Loa's first eruption happened between one million and 700,000 years ago.

WHERE? On Hawaii's Big Island

HOW BIG? This massive volcano is actually over 55,700 ft. tall, but we get to see only 13,000 ft. of the mountain — the bulk of it is below sea level.

WOW FACTOR! It is the biggest volcano in the world and is one of the most active on Earth.

Sun, sand, and waves! That's what most people first picture when they think of Hawaii, one of the most beautiful spots in the world. What you may not know is that Hawaii is not only beautiful, but potentially deadly.

Hawaii is made up of a group of 137 islands. Have you ever thought about how the Hawaiian Islands were formed hundreds of miles off the Pacific coast of North America? They were created by one of the most destructive forces in nature — volcanoes! And when it comes to those lava-spewing spouts, Mauna Loa tops the list as the biggest volcano in the world.

Hawaii is a popular tourist destination. Its warm weather, sandy beaches, unique culture, and beautiful setting are good reasons for a visit. Plus, there's the chance to see volcanoes! But beware, authorities are always monitoring volcanic activity, and scientists predict it is only a matter of time before the sleeping Mauna Loa erupts again. Read on to find out why Mauna Loa flows in to take the #5 spot on our list.

MAUNA LOA

THAT'S INCREDIBLE!

Mauna Loa is one of the most active volcanoes in the world. It has erupted 15 times since 1900! The most recent eruption took place in 1984, so there is a lot of monitoring to look out for signs of unrest or activity in the volcano. Mauna Loa (along with Hawaii's other four volcanoes) is also responsible for the creation and growth of the Hawaiian Islands. Its red hot lava flows into the ocean and creates an ever expanding coastline.

Quick Fact

The word "volcano" comes from the name "Vulcan," the god of fire in Roman mythology. Mauna Loa means "Long Mountain" in the Hawaiian language, probably because of its long, gently sloping shape.

FORCES AT WORK

Eruptions take place when pressure inside Earth forces out molten magma through fissures or cracks in Earth's crust. As layers of cooled lava build up, landforms such as volcanoes are formed. In the case of Mauna Loa, the lava flows out of fissures in the ocean floor, and the layers of lava first form a seamount and then slowly build into a mountain above sea level.

INSIDE OUT

With a volume of 9,700 cubic miles, Mauna Loa is the largest volcano on Earth. It takes up half the area of Hawaii's Big Island and began to form nearly one million years ago. There is a caldera, called Mokuaweoweo, at the summit. Mauna Loa is a shield volcano. It is wider than it is tall and was formed from a large number of slow-moving and fluid lava flows.

fissures: *long cracks producing liquid flows*
caldera: *basin-shaped volcanic depression*

Why do you think people live near volcanoes? Weigh the dangers versus the benefits.

Hawaii is actually made up of five volcanoes which "blend" together because of their closeness to each other, forming one single island. Mauna Loa takes up half of the island's area, making it the biggest volcano in the world (see map).

N

Kohala

Mauna Kea

Hualalai

W

E

Mauna Loa

Kilauea

S

Quick Fact

Active volcanoes are ones that erupt regularly. Dormant volcanoes have not erupted recently, but they are still active. Extinct volcanoes are no longer active.

HOT SPOTS

This theory explains how the Hawaiian Island chain was formed.

During a 1977 eruption, a scientist on Kilauea Volcano gets a close-up view of spewing lava fountains.

In the 1960s, a geophysicist named J. Tuzo Wilson came up with an idea to explain the volcanic activity in the Pacific Ocean, in the middle of the huge Pacific Plate. Scientists thought that volcanoes were only created at plate boundaries and could not explain why they were being created in the middle of a tectonic plate.

Dr. Wilson said that there are "hot spots" under Earth's crust where a lot of heat collects in a small area. The heat makes the rock melt, forming magma. The magma floats to the surface and forces its way out of fissures in the crust. Over time, the continual outpouring of magma forms a seamount (or island volcano if the hot spot is under the ocean floor, as in the case of the Hawaiian Islands). Hot spots never move. As the Pacific Plate moves north over this hot spot, a line of new volcanoes are formed.

Pacific Plate: *hunk of Earth's crust covered by the Pacific Ocean*

If Wilson's theory was true, then the volcanoes in the Hawaiian Island chain should be of different ages, from oldest to youngest in a single direction. Wilson took samples of volcanic rock and tested them. He found the oldest rocks on the northernmost island of Kauai. He also found the rocks got younger as he went south. The youngest rocks were found on the Big Island of Hawaii, the southernmost island.

The Expert Says...

" We don't believe an eruption is right around the corner, but every day that goes by is one day closer to that event. "

— Paul Okubo, seismologist at the Hawaiian Volcano Observatory on Hawaii's Big Island

Take Note

Mauna Loa flows into the #5 spot on our list. It is one of the biggest and most active volcanoes in the world. If it should erupt without warning, the destruction to people, animals, and plants in the surrounding areas would be devastating.

• Why is it important to learn about volcanoes? Make a list of reasons.

5   3   2   1

MAP ILLUSTRATION—BRANDON KÖPKE; SCIENTIST— PHOTO BY J.D. GRIGGS / U.S. GEOLOGICAL SURVEY
ALL OTHER IMAGES–SHUTTERSTOCK,ISTOCKPHOTO

The seafloor's landscape is read by sound beams that transmit echoes. The different colors indicate the different depths of the trench.

WHERE? In the Pacific Ocean off the east coast of Japan, near the Mariana Islands

HOW BIG? Approximately 1,550 mi. long, 42 mi. wide, and 6 mi. deep

WOW FACTOR! The Mariana Trench is where the deepest point of the Earth's crust, called Challenger Deep, is found.

The Mariana Trench is located in the Pacific Ocean, just east of the 14 Mariana Islands, near Japan. Hidden beneath the ocean's surface, this underwater land formation is actually the deepest location on our planet. It is so deep that if you turned Mount Everest, Earth's highest mountain, upside down in the trench, it would still be thousands of miles short of the bottom. So don't try holding your breath for this swim!

What makes this deep-sea abyss even more incredible is the number of amazing organisms and sea creatures that it supports. Explorers and scientists have just begun to explore its endless depths. That's because the crushing pressure of the deep sea makes dives of any kind very difficult. For the time being, we can only piece together the strange reality of ocean life based on the few clues we have uncovered so far. The Mariana Trench remains one of the world's most incredible, and mysterious, land formations. That is why it takes the #4 spot on our list …

abyss: *very deep or bottomless ditch*

MARIANA TRENCH

THAT'S INCREDIBLE!

The Mariana Trench was first discovered and surveyed in 1951 by a British ship called *Challenger*. That's where the name Challenger Deep comes from. It describes the deepest point on our planet. This underwater abyss is home to a variety of marine life, most of which we have never seen. We know that some of the marine organisms get nutrients from hot springs found at the bottom of the trench. Earth's oceans are so dark and deep that scientists know less about them than they do about outer space. Studying the organisms that can survive in the trench's harsh conditions is also helping scientists to figure out where in space life might exist.

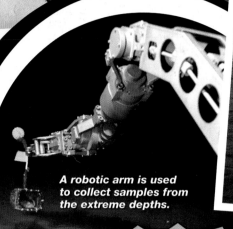

A robotic arm is used to collect samples from the extreme depths.

The Japanese submersible KAIKO is used to explore and photograph the trench.

? Do you think it is more important to explore the ocean depths or deep space? Explain.

Quick Fact

At a depth of 490 feet, little light exists along the ocean floor and colors are no longer visible to the human eye. This lack of light makes life very rare because without sunlight, there is no energy supplied to initiate a food chain.

FORCES AT WORK

The trench was formed by subduction. This happens when forces inside Earth cause two tectonic plates in the ocean to move and collide with each other. This collision forced the edge of the Pacific Plate to subduct, or go underneath, the edge of the Philippine Plate.

INSIDE OUT

The Mariana Trench is the deepest part of Earth's oceans. The world's oceans represent 80 percent of the biosphere. That makes it the largest habitat for creatures on the planet. The ocean floor is covered with an "ooze" that is made up of shells, animal skeletons, and decaying plants.

subduction: *movement of one tectonic plate beneath another*
biosphere: *part of Earth and its atmosphere where life can exist*

Mariana Trench

Philippine Plate

Pacific Plate

Subduction

Volcanic vents let out smoke and volcanic ash. They heat up the water near them so life can survive.

How Deep Is the Ocean?

An article from
Canada & the World Backgrounder,
January 1, 2005

White crabs feeding on poisonous chemicals — bon appétit!

When Irving Berlin wrote the lyrics to "How Deep Is the Ocean?" in 1932, the answer wasn't known. Today, we know; it varies.

The deepest parts of the ocean are deep-sea trenches. These are generally off the continental shelves and plunge as much as 11 kilometers [6 miles]. The deepest point is 11,033 meters [6,855 miles] below the surface in the Mariana Trench in the Pacific Ocean.

Only in recent years have we developed technologies that will get us to the deepest parts of the oceans and back again alive. Not surprisingly, not much is known about what happens down there. What is known is bizarre.

Tubeworms

On the deep ocean floor scientists have found hydrothermal vents. From these vents a toxic brew of superheated water, hydrogen sulphide gas, and heavy metals bubbles forth. The pressure at these depths would crush humans as flat as a sheet of paper, and there is no light.

In this harshest of environments several hundred life-forms exist, about 95 percent of them unknown until the 1980s. There are tubeworms, blind shrimps, and giant white crabs. These unique creatures seem to find poisonous chemicals yummy enough to survive on through a process called chemosynthesis.

hydrothermal: *pertaining to hot water produced by Earth's internal heat*
chemosynthesis: *process of creating energy from chemical compounds*

? Find out where the hot springs on the ocean floor come from and what makes the water so hot.

Quick Fact

The highest temperature that bacteria living in the trench can withstand is 235.4°F. The highest temperature that any animal we know on Earth can withstand is only 122°F.

bacteria: *life-forms made of single cells that lack a nucleus*

The Expert Says...

" The Mariana Trench fascinates a lot of people. ... It caught my attention when they found small fungi there. ... "

— Angelina Souren, geologist and marine biogeochemist

fungi: *classification of plants that include mushrooms, yeasts, and molds*

Take Note

The Mariana Trench is one of a kind. It is a unique land formation that gives us the deepest known spot in the world. The fact that it is able to support life-forms adds to its mysterious and unique quality. It takes the #4 spot on our list.
• Do you think the Mariana Trench would be higher up on our list if we knew more about it? Explain why or why not.

5   **4**   3   2   1

GRAND CANYON—MIKE QUINN/NPS

Long before the Grand Canyon was first explored in 1869, it was inhabited by Native Americans who built settlements within the canyon walls and its many caves.

ON

WHERE? Grand Canyon National Park in Arizona, United States

HOW BIG? It is about 280 mi. long, ranges from 0.3 to 15 mi. wide, and is 5,245 ft. deep in some spots.

WOW FACTOR! Believe it or not! Water was responsible for creating this deep large crack in the landscape.

To see the Grand Canyon for the first time is an experience few people will forget. Its unimaginable size, deep color, and ancient rock layers are quite unlike any other natural land formation on Earth.

Half of Earth's history lies in the canyon's rocks. The oldest and deepest rock layer began forming about two billion years ago. The different layers of rock give clues about how the landscape has changed over the years. They tell of mountains that moved, of ancient oceans that poured across the land, of deserts, swamps, and rivers that once existed — all where the canyon now lies.

The canyon itself is a steep-sided gorge carved by the mighty Colorado River. From the base of the canyon, you can look up the high walls that rise about 6,000 feet from the river, a visual record of the six million years it took to form the canyon.

As one of the seven natural wonders of the world, the Grand Canyon shows an impressive display of erosion and Earth's natural beauty. That is why it takes the #3 spot on our list ...

---

gorge: *narrow pássage between hills, often containing a ravine or stream*

GRAND CANYON

THAT'S INCREDIBLE!

The Grand Canyon is one of the most studied land formations in the world. It has a rich fossil record, is home to a collection of geologic features and rock types, and has numerous caves. Because the Grand Canyon is part of the Colorado River Basin, water flows into this area after rainfalls. This makes erosion a continuing process and allows 2,500 different types of vegetation to grow. Some examples are the ponderosa pine, fernbush, and banana yucca.

Quick Fact

You can get to the floor of the valley by hiking down the canyon, riding a mule, rafting from upriver, or taking a boat down.

FORCES AT WORK

At one time, this area was covered by a body of water. Millions of years passed and the water disappeared, leaving behind many layers of sedimentary rock. Then Earth's plates shifted and the Colorado River began to flow through here. The river started to wear away the sedimentary rock. As more millions of years passed, the river's course changed several times and widened the size of the canyon. After many more million years, Earth's plates started to rise. This and the power of erosion created a deeper gorge, which gradually became the canyon we see today.

? Fossils of marine life have been found inside the Grand Canyon. Why is this important to geologists?

INSIDE OUT

Because the Grand Canyon is so deep and so eroded, a variety of rocks are exposed. Researchers have uncovered 10 main layers of rock, each one different from its neighbor. Most of the rocks are sedimentary. Some of the top layers contain limestone and sandstone, which erode easily. Lava, a harder volcanic rock, is found in the western end of the canyon.

? The path of the Colorado River has changed several times over the course of history. If the river's path were to change again, how do you think the area would be affected?

Slicing the Sky

Anyone who is looking for a more panoramic view of the Grand Canyon can now do it easily — by taking a stroll on the all-glass Skywalk. Read this article to get the full scoop.

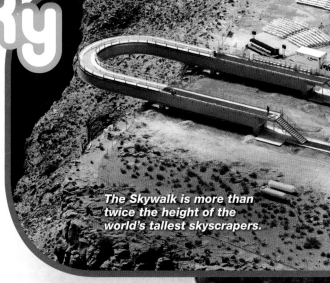

The Skywalk is more than twice the height of the world's tallest skyscrapers.

Commissioned by the Hualapai Indian tribe who owns the land, this bridge is the first of its kind. It hangs more than 6,000 feet above the canyon's floor and extends almost 70 feet from the canyon's rim. Only a few sheets of glass stand between visitors and a free fall to the bottom.

Building this all-glass Skywalk was an engineering feat. The structure is built to withstand tornado-like vertical winds whipping up at 86 mph. To secure the bridge into place, it has been cantilevered atop the cliff with 94 steel rods drilled 45 feet deep into the limestone rock. The bridge supports 70 tons, equal to the weight of about 700 people. But this will never have to be tested; the maximum occupancy is 120 people. To keep the Skywalk from vibrating, three steel plates weighing 3,195 pounds each have been placed inside the hollow bridge. They will act as shock absorbers, moving up and down to counteract the vibrations from traffic and wind gusts. For extra support, the walkway is made from three-inch-thick glass that is heat-strengthened and enclosed with glass walls.

Shoe covers are given out so people don't slip or scratch the glass.

commissioned: *ordered to be built or produced*
cantilevered: *anchored at one end and projected into an open space*

The Expert Says...

" The glories and the beauties of form, color, and sound unite in the Grand Canyon ... "

— John Wesley Powell, American explorer

Take Note

A list of the world's most amazing landforms must include the Grand Canyon. It takes our #3 spot. Millions of people visit it every year to admire its vast size, its beautiful landscape, and its amazing rock formations. Plus, with the new Skywalk, you can get a closer view of its rocks and landforms.

• Aside from sightseeing, you can also hike, run, go whitewater rafting, or take a tour on the Skywalk. Which would appeal to you most? Explain.

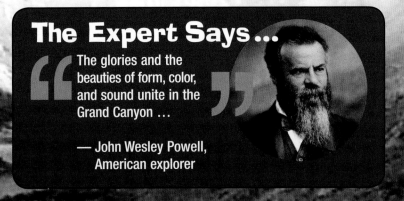

5   4   **3**   2   1

② THE ANDES

The Andes mountain range is divided into three sections: the Southern Andes in Argentina and Chile, the Central Andes in Chile and Peru, and the Northern Andes in Venezuela, Colombia, and Ecuador.

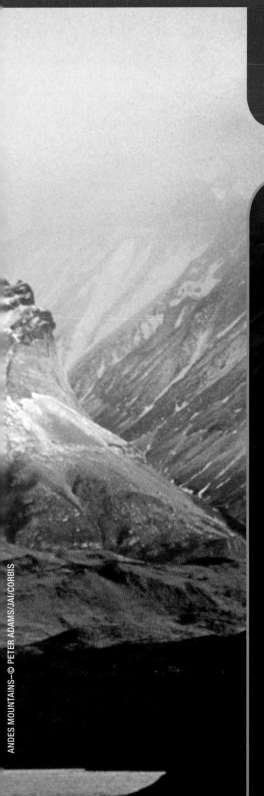

WHERE? Along the entire west coast of South America between Argentina and Chile

HOW BIG? 4,350 mi. long and 310 mi. wide

WOW FACTOR! This is the longest mountain range in the world.

As mountains were being created millions of years ago, Earth's tectonic plates collided and created a natural wall of rock. This wall acts as a barrier blocking most of South America from the Pacific Ocean.

Today, this wall is called the Andes — the longest mountain range in the world, running for 4,350 miles from north to south along the west coast of South America. The range is so long it runs through seven different countries: Argentina, Chile, Bolivia, Peru, Ecuador, Colombia, and Venezuela. In comparison, the Himalayas in Asia run through six countries and only measure about 1,500 miles long. The Andes are also home to some of the highest peaks in the world, which average 13,120 feet high.

The Andes have some of the most spectacular scenery in the world. They also have many different climate zones and rare species of wildlife, such as the condor, flamingo, Andean iguana, giant toad, mountain lion, llama, and many other rare plants and birds. These mountains are so long and stretch so far that it is possible to ski on the western slopes in below zero weather and trek through tropical rain forests all in the same day. How can it possibly get any better than that?

The Andes mountain range is visible from outer space, so it's no wonder it attracts tourists from all over the world. It is definitely one of our planet's greatest landforms and it takes the #2 spot on our list.

THE ANDES

THAT'S INCREDIBLE!

The Andes mountain range provides one of the most breathtaking sights from the sky, ranging from rain forests, to snow-capped mountains, to volcanoes. It also offers unforgettable hiking and climbing opportunities. But what is more amazing is that millions of people live in different parts of this mountain range. The populations are mainly concentrated in cities and villages in the lush lowlands, but many also settle in remote and even barren lands higher up on the mountains. Tobacco, cotton, coffee, and cocoa are important crops in the region.

Quick Fact

The Andes mountain system is the source of many rivers, including the Amazon and Pilcomayo.

FORCES AT WORK

The Andes formed about 100 million years ago because of Earth's shifting tectonic plates. The Pacific Plate started to move underneath the South American Plate and lifted its outer edge, resulting in the Andes mountain range. Aconcagua, the highest mountain peak in the Andes, is almost 22,965 feet above sea level. That's nearly twice as tall as the highest mountain in the Rockies!

? As the Andes mountains are continually exposed to the powerful forces of erosion, they are slowly being worn away. What do you think is going to be the fate of these mountains another hundred million years from now?

INSIDE OUT

All three types of rock can be found in the immense Andes mountain range. The main type of rock in the mountains is sedimentary. There is also igneous rock, which was formed by lava flows from volcanic eruptions. As tectonic plates collided, the intense heat and pressure also created metamorphic rock.

Quick Fact

People are damaging the Andes' ecosystem by cutting down trees and mining for gold, silver, and copper in these mountains. Many rare animals and plant life are also in danger of being destroyed because of human interference.

Seen here from a satellite, the snow-capped Andes span the west side of South America from Argentina to Chile.

SURVIVING THE ANDES

This true account tells the story of 16 brave survivors who crashed into the Andes.

On October 12, 1972, a plane carrying an amateur rugby team from Uruguay left for Santiago, Chile. To get there they had to fly over the snow-covered Andes mountains.

Everything seemed fine until they hit bad weather. The plane crashed into the side of a mountain losing both wings and the tail. It ended up landing on its belly, surrounded by snow and mountains. The roof of the plane was white, making it blend in with the snow and harder to spot from above. To make matters worse, it was bitterly cold and the passengers didn't have many extra clothes. Rescue parties stopped looking after only eight days.

Thirty-two of the 45 passengers survived the crash. Without proper medical attention, some of the injured died. All the 28 survivors had to eat was chocolate, crackers, jam, and wine. As everyone grew weaker, they realized the only way to survive would be to eat the remains of the dead.

To make matters worse, on the 17th day there was an avalanche. Several more people died; only 19 remained. By this point, some of the survivors decided the only way they would make it out alive was if they took action themselves. Three survivors decided to walk their way out of the Andes.

After 10 days of walking through some of the highest mountains in the world, they came across a Chilean rancher in a valley. On December 21, 1972, 70 days after the crash, they were led out of the valley and taken back to civilization. Only 16 survivors were rescued.

Photo taken just before the survivors of the Andes plane crash were rescued.

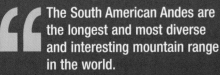 How do you feel about the survivors' choice? What would you have done in this situation?

The Expert Says...

"The South American Andes are the longest and most diverse and interesting mountain range in the world."

— Gregory Knapp, professor, University of Texas at Austin

Take Note

As the longest and one of the highest mountain ranges in the world, the Andes deserve the #2 spot on our list. They pass through seven different countries with varying landscapes, wildlife, temperatures, and environments.

• Research the different climates of the Andes mountains. Which climate would you want to live in and why?

5   4   3   **2**   1

The Nile River Delta flows from south to north and opens into the Mediterranean Sea.

NILE RIVER DELTA—© CORBIS

DELTA

WHERE? Northern Egypt, stretching from Alexandria in the west to Port Said in the east

HOW BIG? About 110 mi. long and 160 mi. wide

WOW FACTOR! The Nile River Delta is the largest in the world.

The Nile River Delta is where civilization began in ancient Egypt. This delta, located at the mouth of the Nile River, is the largest in the world. It is built up from layers of sediments — soil, sand, and minerals — that are washed from the land and carried by the Nile River as it flows through central Africa all the way north to the Mediterranean Sea.

The soil in the delta is some of the most fertile in the world. It is very rich in minerals that are natural fertilizers for crops. The fertile soil and the warm Mediterranean climate allow farmers to plant and harvest three crops a year, providing lots of food for people who live in the delta and surrounding areas.

People have lived and farmed along the Nile and on the Nile River Delta at least 5,000 years. Settlements have grown into cities as millions of people have flocked to the delta to live and work. This is why some people believe the Nile River Delta is where one of the first civilizations began. Today, it is still the hub of Egypt and it is our #1 choice for the most incredible landform in the world.

sediments: soil, sand, and minerals washed from the land into the water

THAT'S INCREDIBLE!

The Nile River Delta was actually responsible for the development of the ancient Egyptian civilization. The delta area became the breadbasket of Egypt, a place where people settled and where the great Egyptian civilization began. Before the construction of the Aswan High Dam in 1971, the flooding of the Nile was predictable enough for the Egyptians to plan their yearly crops around it. The Nile River Delta is an important stopover place for millions of birds that fly between Europe and Africa every year. It is also the winter home to thousands of waterbirds, such as the little gull, whiskered tern, and cormorant.

Quick Fact

The Nile River Delta was named by early geographers because its triangular shape reminded them of the Greek letter "delta."

FORCES AT WORK

The Nile River carries large amounts of sediments from the mountains and surrounding lands as it flows north into the Mediterranean Sea. Flood waters add to the sediment loads, which are deposited at the river's mouth. Smaller rivers, called tributaries, run off the main river into the delta area. These tributaries help spread the load of sediments over a wider area. Over time, the deposits of sediments create a delta, which is a triangular shape with a very broad base that opens into the sea.

INSIDE OUT

The Nile River Delta is made up of sediments that have been deposited by the Nile River over millions of years. The Nile's beds are built up from sediment particles. The size of these particles depends on the flow of water. Where water flows fast, the particle size tends to be big and coarse. When the flow slows down, the grains become small and fine. Because the sediment gets smaller as the flow slows down, only the larger particles are left behind. This cycle creates different sediment beds.

Quick Fact

The top layer of soil on the delta is called black loam, which is very rich in minerals and nutrients and is an excellent food for crops.

Farmers along the Nile River Delta dig channels to divert flood waters to irrigate their crops.

CRADLE OF CIVILIZATION

This report details the changes that are taking place in the Nile River Delta.

Ever since ancient times, the Nile River has been a vital source of food and water. The river carries almost 140 million tons of fertile volcanic soil that flows in from the Ethiopian highlands and deposits them on the plains as it makes its way to the delta. Most of Egypt's population live in the delta region, which has up to 620 people in each square mile of land.

The annual flooding of the river used to be one of the most important events in the life of the people. However, the construction of the Aswan High Dam and Lake Nasser in 1971 put a stop to the annual flooding. As a result, the delta no longer receives an annual supply of nutrients and sediments from upstream. This has lowered the quality of the floodplain's soils, creating a need for fertilizers.

The Aswan High Dam cuts off and regulates much of the water flow to the Nile River Delta.

The dam is also causing the delta's outer edges to wear away because sediments no longer reach it. Salt levels are rising because its connection to the Mediterranean Sea is getting bigger. This is hurting fish and plant species in the delta and surrounding areas. While the area continues to be used for farming and agriculture, water flow is now controlled by the dam instead of the yearly floods.

? The dam generates hydroelectricity and the lake stores water that can be used for irrigation. Do you think these advantages outweigh the disadvantages? Should the Aswan High Dam have been built? Research to support your position.

The Expert Says...

" Fifteen percent of the delta could be lost by the year 2100 … It's a scary prospect. "

— Danie Stanley, geologist

? Do you share the geologist's concern? What would be the impact of losing 15 percent of the delta?

Take Note

As the only landform that is directly responsible for the development of a great ancient civilization, the Nile River Delta takes the top spot on our list. It affects the history and lives of many millions of people in Egypt and it provides habitats for rare species of wildlife.
• How do you think the Nile River Delta's relationship with people sets it apart from the other land formations on our list?

5   4   3   2   1

We Thought ...

Here are the criteria we used in ranking the 10 most incredible landforms.

The landform:
- Is especially large in size
- Is unique among other land formations
- Has a major impact on the environment
- Has a major impact on people
- Was formed in an unusual way
- Teaches us about the history of Earth
- Is an amazing sight to see
- Offers a habitat for rare life-forms

What Do You Think?

1. Do you agree with our ranking? If you don't, try ranking them yourself. Justify your ranking with data from your own research and reasoning. You may refer to our criteria, or you may want to draw up your own list of criteria.

2. Here are three other landforms that we considered but in the end did not include in our top 10 list: Sahara Desert, the Great Barrier Reef, and the Canadian Shield.
   • Find out more about them. Do you think they should have made our list? Give reasons for your response.
   • Are there other landforms that you think should have made our list? Explain your choices.

Index